Lessons from the Freiburg School

The Institutional Foundations of Freedom and Prosperity

CIS occasional papers 44

Lessons from the Freiburg School

The Institutional Foundations of Freedom and Prosperity

Wolfgang Kasper and Manfred Streit

THE CENTRE FOR
INDEPENDENT
STUDIES

1993

Published July 1993 by

The Centre for Independent Studies Limited

National Library of Australia

Cataloguing-in-Publication Data:

    Kasper, Wolfgang., 1939-
    Lessons from the Freiburg School.

    Bibliography.
    ISBN 0 949769 88 6.

    1. Liberalism. 2. Liberalism – Australia.
    3. Liberalism – Germany. I. Streit, Manfred E.
    II. Centre for Independent Studies (Australia).
    III. Title. (Series : CIS occasional papers ; 44)

320.51

Printed by Australian Print Group

Contents

Foreword

It is widely recognised that Australia will have to undertake further comprehensive reforms in the 1990s to unlock its considerable economic potential and to avert the growing disillusionment and alienation of young people with a *dirigiste* economic and political regime that leaves them too few freedoms and opportunities.

Of the many experiments with comprehensive reform, we should better acquaint ourselves with the West German reforms that Economics Minister Ludwig Erhard implemented in the late 1940s and 1950s, since these reforms produced a durable success. The Centre for Independent Studies is therefore pleased to publish this Occasional Paper, which shows the relevance of the intellectual foundations of the German reform program. These were laid by a group of economists, lawyers and social philosophers who were centred on Freiburg University and who became known as the 'Freiburg School'.

In the face of the failure of the Weimar Republic and the rise of National Socialism, the members of the Freiburg School went back to the liberal principles of the writers of the Scottish Enlightenment such as David Hume and Adam Smith, and adapted their ideas to a modern industrial society with its pressure groups and the temptations of redistributionist politics. The Freiburg School concluded that certain fundamental institutions were crucial to shaping individual decision-making and therefore prosperity. They argued that the state, through the law, had the task of maintaining and defending basic institutions such as property rights, free competition, stable money and liability for the consequences of one's free decisions. Majority rule and mere hopes for a spontaneous order alone would not suffice to guarantee a durable free order.

German *ordo* liberalism differs from the British, American and Australian liberal traditions in that it puts more faith in constitutional law to safeguard basic freedoms and in well-designed government institutions to create a durable framework for a free and prospering society. This is of course an arguable position, but the historic German success adds some weight to the 'Freiburg position'. Although the welfare state and industrial pressures gradually eroded the *ordo* liberal concept in Germany after the mid-1960s and led to a slide into the 'social market economy' and poor growth, Germany still has some institutions which are based on *ordo* liberalism and which are sources of enduring resilience. In view of the ease and speed with which collectivist conservative politicians emasculated the Reagan and

Thatcher reforms, and given the inconsistencies and costly reversals of the New Zealand reforms after 1985, it may indeed be useful to discuss an institutional-legal underpinning of reforms in Australia and New Zealand. The concepts of *ordo* liberalism offer inspiration for durable and effective reform.

Much will depend on whether Australian and New Zealand reformers will be able to concentrate on the fundamentals needed to underpin a free and spontaneously prospering society. This will require clear leadership and modesty as to what politicians and collective action can achieve. It will also require that people of good will concentrate their efforts on discussing not so much whether government is good or bad, but what constitutes good government.

For all this, the policy-tested ideas of the Freiburg School can offer some direction and inspiration. The Centre for Independent Studies is pleased to present this introduction to a body of liberal ideas that is not well enough known in this part of the world. It is written by Wolfgang Kasper of the University of New South Wales, a long-time associate of the CIS and an advocate of comprehensive reform in Australia and New Zealand, and by his friend and colleague of many years, Manfred Streit, who now holds the chair in economics at Freiburg University held by F.A. Hayek in the 1960s. It is a modest but effective summary of some of the major ideas of the Freiburg school and is a good start to a more comprehensive examination of *ordo* liberal ideas and their applicability to the political economy of Australia and New Zealand.

Greg Lindsay

About the Authors

Wolfgang Kasper, born in 1939, is a Professor of Economics at the University of New South Wales (Australian Defence Force Academy campus). After formative years in post-war Germany and elsewhere in Europe, he earned degrees in Modern Languages (English, Spanish) and Economics, including his PhD. He then worked for the German Council of Economic Advisors, the Kiel Institute of World Economics, the Malaysian Minister of Finance, and the Australian National University. He also served with the Reserve Bank of Australia and OECD, Paris.

Now an Australian citizen by choice, he has done scholarly research and practical consultancy work for government and industry on a wide range of policy problems, such as long-term growth, industrial innovation, Australian R&D strategies, industrial structural change, the economies of Australia, East Asia and Fiji, and the international mobility of people, capital and technical know-how (globalisation). He is the author or principal editor of about ten books and 100 learned articles, and writes occasional commentaries in the press. He serves on the Advisory Council of the Centre for Independent Studies. His publications for the CIS include *Capital Xenophobia: Australia's Controls of Foreign Investment* (1984), *Fiji: Opportunity from Adversity?* (1988; co-authored with Jeff Bennett and Richard Blandy), and *Aid and Development in the South Pacific* (1991; co-authored with Peter Bauer and Savenaca Siwatibau). He has also contributed to *Policy*, the quarterly journal of the CIS.

Manfred E. Streit, born in 1939, is Professor of Economics in Freiburg University, Germany, where he holds the chair previously occupied by Friedrich von Hayek and where Walter Eucken, a founder of the *ordo* liberal school, once taught. He is also the Director of the free-market Institute of Economic Research at Freiburg University.

He completed his formal education in Germany with an economics degree and a PhD from the University of the Saar. He then worked as a research assistant in the university, on the staff of the German Council of Economic Advisors, as a Lecturer in Economics at Reading University, UK, as a professor in Mannheim University, Germany, and at the European University Institute in Florence. Since 1990, he has been a Professor in Freiburg. He also held visiting positions at Queen's University, Canada (in 1969) and the Australian National University, Canberra (in 1979). He serves on various scientific and policy-advisory boards in Europe, including the Advisory Council of Germany's Ministry of Economics.

His record of academic teaching and research ranges from spatial economics and the functioning of futures markets, to principles of policy-making and research on a liberal economic order for the integrating European Community. He is the author of a well-known German textbook on political economy.

The authors have maintained a dialogue with each other since they were students at the University of the Saar and worked on the staff of the German Council of Economic Advisors in the 1960s. Both are members of the Mont Pèlerin Society.

Acknowledgements

The authors wish to thank Peter Bernholz (Basel, Switzerland and Canberra), Chandran Kukathas (Canberra) and Wilfried Schulz (Munich, Germany) as well as two anonymous referees for helpful comments, without, however, implicating them in any way in their conclusions.

Lessons from the Freiburg School

The Institutional Foundations
of Freedom and Prosperity

Wolfgang Kasper and Manfred Streit

I.   INTRODUCTION

In recent years, the 'Freiburg School' of law and economics, which developed a specifically German brand of liberalism, known as '*ordo* liberalism', between the 1930s and the 1950s, has attracted growing international attention. A representative sample of the key writings of the Freiburg School has been published in English for the first time in the late 1980s (Peacock & Willgerodt, 1989a) and the Freiburg contribution has been discussed widely from an Anglo-Saxon view point (Peacock & Willgerodt, 1989b). Many reformers in Eastern Europe are now looking to the Freiburg School's ideas about a free and effective socio-economic system.

The Freiburgers — so named because the central concepts of German neo-liberalism were developed in the University of Freiburg in south-west Germany — drew on the basic philosophy of the Scottish Enlightenment to develop a liberal policy design for a modern industrial democracy. They stressed the importance of underlying institutional and legal arrangements for sustaining freedom and prosperity. They distinguished between competitive market **processes** and the institutional **framework** ('order') within which markets function: which is why they called themselves *ordo* liberals. The *ordo* liberal position was that the government should help to shape and defend the social and economic order, but should leave the market processes to competing individuals. The concept of order thus refers to the set of rules that constrain individual economic behaviour, and to an approach to policy making that sets down general rules, but does not attend to specific consequences and outcomes. If, for example, a competitor prices himself out of the market, it is not the responsibility of government to attend to the consequent unemployment. 'Order' of course embraces unplanned, informal ordering norms (like ethical rules) that may evolve in the light of experience, and rules that are designed by legislation. The German

1

neo-liberals focused primarily on the formal legal-institutional aspects, and on how different styles of legislation and regulation affect economic prosperity and individual freedom.

Early Anglo-Saxon Reactions to *Ordo* Liberalism

Ordo liberalism was highly influential in shaping the economic and social policies of West Germany in the late 1940s and 1950s. Yet, although it formed the intellectual basis for West Germany's post-war economic success, it remained largely an academic product that was not traded internationally. This had a lot to do with the prevailing international intellectual fashion in the 1950s and 1960s, which favoured Keynesian demand management and selective interventionism where 'market failures' were diagnosed. The *ordo* liberal preoccupation with underlying institutional arrangements, like property rights, genuine competition and the rule of law, and the effect of these arrangements on the supply side of the economy, was largely dismissed internationally as idiosyncratic at best and economically dangerous at worst. When one of the central works of the Freiburg School — Eucken's *Foundations of Economics* — was published in Britain in 1950, an anonymous reviewer in the *Times Literary Supplement* held Eucken responsible 'for mass unemployment and social inequality unparalleled even under the Nazis' (Eucken, 1992:2), and prominent Oxford economist Thomas (later Lord) Balogh castigated Erhard's reforms aiming at a smoothly functioning market system as dangerous and irresponsible (Balogh, 1950).

Admittedly, for a considerable time the Germans did not absorb Keynesianism, partly because the *ordo* liberals had cautioned against artificial demand stimulation on the grounds that such policies would gradually erode a liberal economic order based on the responsibility of the individual and spontaneous, self-correcting processes (Eucken, in Peacock & Willgerodt, 1989a:43–5). Now, of course, we know that they were far ahead of their time in pointing out that demand stimulation erodes long-term job creation and undermines the rules that make for long-term stability. Instead of following the fashion of the 1950s, at a time when most other nations fought supposed 'secular stagnation' and the perceived dangers of unemployment with loose fiscal and monetary policies, West German economic policy concentrated on freeing up markets, maintaining a stable currency and pursuing conservative fiscal and monetary policies. German policy concentrated on making the supply apparatus responsive to market changes by creating a favourable framework for individual initiative, drawing heavily on the teachings of the *ordo* liberals. This proved a resounding success: Between 1950 and 1960, real output in West Germany more than doubled (8.8 per cent growth annually), total employment went from 20 to 25 million, the number of unemployed fell from 1.9 million to less than 300 000 despite a massive influx of refugees and the return of prisoners of war; labour productivity rose on average by 5.7 per cent annually. Ten years after the introduction of the new deutschmark currency and an independent central bank in 1948, full international currency convertibility could be introduced. Capital could again be moved into and out of Germany without government controls, and Germany was able to promote international-trade liberalisation by unilateral tariff cuts. Most foreign observers failed to see the close connection between the simple, reliable competitive order and the commitment to a stable currency based on central-bank independence on the one hand and the new-found dynamic efficiency of the German economy on the other. Most preferred not to treat the evidence seriously, consigning it instead to the realm of the irrational and labelling it an 'economic miracle'. Relatively few writers bothered to explain Germany's institutional innovations to the outside world (the exceptions include Sohmen, 1959, and Erhard, 1960).

The Belated International Discovery of *Ordo* Liberalism

Matters have changed greatly since then. The breakdown of socialism and the ensuing struggle to transform the failed socialist system have focused renewed attention on economic systems. The *ordo* liberal focus on the functional properties of society's institutional arrangements attracts growing attention among the reformers who are trying to come to grips with the transformation in eastern Europe. In the West, the creeping failure of democratic societies with long-standing market economies — from the United States to Australia — has given rise to renewed questioning about the institutional underpinnings of individual economic activity (for example Hayek, 1979; Buchanan, 1988). The initial thrust of microeconomic reform has been to cut back the influence of the government. But increasing attention is moving from the negative message — reduction of state influence — to the search for a positive message — what roles the state must fulfil in a free, prospering society.

It is becoming increasingly obvious that the capitalist market economy will not deliver the desired results in terms of individual opportunity, material security and independence and an overall dynamic performance unless the basic institutional underpinnings are repaired and unless the system, which has been gradually obliterated by cumulative legislative and regulatory interventions, is simplified and liberalised. Numerous political efforts are now under way to renew the system by creating consistent frameworks of institutions and rules that are more conducive to self-reliance, competition and economic dynamism. In the fast-growing East Asian economies, the 'soft' institutional infrastructure that reconciles individual rivalry with social cohesion by well-understood, shared rules has received considerable attention. A growing number of observers (for example, Chen, 1988; Kasper, 1990) are stressing the importance of a 'neo-Confucian economic order' for rapid economic development and for the reduction of social conflict.

Worldwide moves to transform and reform economic systems (Scobie & Lim, 1992) therefore have much to gain from the earlier, and policy-tested, intellectual work of the German neo-liberals.

II. THE FREIBURG SCHOOL[1]

The Leading Members

The neo-liberal Freiburg School developed its initial intellectual thrust from the spontaneous cooperation of economists and lawyers who happened to join the University of Freiburg in the 1930s. They shared certain views about the serious economic failures of the Weimar Republic and soon developed shared (hostile) attitudes to the Nazi regime. The Freiburg jurists and economists discovered that they shared a commitment to liberty from which sprang similar methodological positions, and they chose complementary research topics.

One central figure who had come to Freiburg in the late 1920s was the economist **Walter Eucken** (1891–1950), the son of the philosopher and Literature Nobel Prize winner, Rudolf Eucken. The younger Eucken's early academic work was inevitably influenced by the

---

1. For more detail of the theoretical and methodological foundations of the Freiburg School and its development since the 1930s, see Streit, 1992b. In this essay, 'Freiburg School' relates primarily to the social scientists working at Freiburg University. After World War II, the Freiburg philosophy gained many followers in other parts of Europe, mainly the German-speaking countries. This group is sometimes labelled 'the Freiburg School', but should more accurately be called either 'the *ordo* liberals' or 'the German neo-liberals'. As this essay makes clear, it is wrong to equate (as some British writers do) *ordo* liberal **theory** with the **practice** of the 'social market policy' which was developed in Germany, especially after the mid–1960s, and which many *ordo* liberals have opposed.

Historical School then dominant in Germany.[2] Yet even his early (1923) study of the German inflation problem already documents a commitment to clear theoretical analysis. To him, it was unacceptable that economists of the Historical School had nothing to offer by way of explanation and policy advice during the German hyper-inflation after World War I. Eucken continued his research in monetary theory, frequently drawing out the implications of his research for applied monetary policy. His theory of interest and capital (1934) was based on the analyses by the Austrian economist Eugen von Böhm-Bawerk and the Swedish economist Knut Wicksell.

In 1933, **Hans Grossmann-Doerth** (1894–1944) joined the Freiburg faculty as a professor of civil and commercial law. Soon after his arrival, he and Eucken initiated a joint seminar in law and economics dealing primarily with problems of the underlying economic order and its legal underpinnings. Not only students but other professors attended the seminar. It became the organisational nucleus of the Freiburg School until political pressure forced it to close in 1936. This did not prevent the members of the seminar from meeting in private, continuing their opposition to the Nazi regime and making plans for the period after its demise.

The third central personality of the Freiburg School was **Franz Böhm** (1895–1977). He came to the faculty from service as a public prosecutor and in the Cartel Office of the Ministry of Economics at Berlin. Eucken and Grossmann-Doerth had been appointed to assess his thesis on competition and monopolisation (1933), which was to gain him access to a university career. Böhm stayed at Freiburg as an assistant professor until 1936, when he moved to Jena. In 1939 he was dismissed from university service for his criticism of the regime's policy towards Jewish fellow citizens. After a trial, he was reinstated, but forbidden to teach. He returned to Freiburg in 1945, became a full professor and served as Vice-President of the university before moving to Frankfurt in 1946. He kept close contact with Freiburg and Eucken, with whom he founded the yearbook *Ordo*, which is still a focal European platform for research on problems of economic order and the institutional framework of a free society.

The Freiburg School attracted a number of bright scholars and

---

2. The German Historical School advocated the recording of historic detail and was critical of using theoretical abstraction to uncover general laws of economic behaviour. It rejected the normative approach to economics that considers economic policy as a means of attaining such values as freedom or growing prosperity.

established an intellectual network in Germany and beyond. Among them was the economist **Friedrich A. Lutz**, who started as an assistant of Eucken, and later made important contributions to the theory and policy of money, business cycles and exchange rates. **Karl Friedrich Maier** excelled in the field of balance-of-payments and monetary theory and contributed original insights into the coordination of economic plans at the micro-level. **Paul Hensel** established himself with innovative research on comparative economic systems, a tradition that was extended to the New Institutional Economics (for English translations and comment on these scholars see Peacock & Willgerodt, 1989a, 1989b). Most of these scholars, together with Eucken and Böhm, made important academic contributions to the design of economic policy in post-war Germany and were in close contact with the economics minister, **Ludwig Erhard**, a fellow neo-liberal and the deft practitioner of economic reform. In the 1950s, the Freiburgers and their allies were thus able to make public and apply the intellectual capital that had been accumulated before and during the Nazi era.

Erhard, who had written as early as 1943/44 about economic policy after a lost war, was doubtless at one with his friends in Freiburg when in 1958 he wrote:

> First consideration must be given to the freedom of every citizen to live his life according to his financial circumstances, personal desires and values. This basic principle of freedom for the consumer must logically be counter-balanced by freedom for the producer to make and sell what he believes to be marketable. . . Freedom for the consumer and freedom to work must be explicitly recognised as inviolable basic rights. . . To offend against them should be regarded as an outrage against society. These principles can only be put into practice if public opinion is prepared to give them priority over any selfish sectoral interests. (Erhard, 1960:6–8)

The Freiburg economists and lawyers had close scholarly contacts with like-minded intellectuals abroad (Luigi Einaudi in Italy, Frank H. Knight and Ludwig von Mises in the United States, Lionel Robbins in England and Jacques Rueff in France). The School even managed to keep open some scientific lines of communication to friends abroad during the politically difficult years. And some German economists, who had fled from the Third Reich, particularly **Wilhelm Röpke** (1948, 1957, 1960, 1963) and **Alexander Rüstow** (1980), remained close to Eucken and Böhm. After 1945, these economists welcomed the opportunity to strengthen their intellectual and personal ties with the

Freiburg liberals. When Friedrich A. von Hayek (1899–1992) initiated the Mont Pèlerin Society in 1947 as a forum for the renaissance of classical liberalism under modern conditions, Eucken was invited to join, and Franz Böhm soon also became a member.

In 1950, Eucken died in London, where he was delivering an invited lecture series at the London School of Economics (Eucken, 1951). In the 1960s, twelve years after Eucken's death, Hayek left Chicago to join the Faculty in Freiburg. He openly considered himself as a successor of his late friend Walter Eucken, despite the fact that he held different views on a number of fundamental theoretical positions, for example on the role of man-made laws as against spontaneous order and the *ordo* liberals' belief in what collective action by government can achieve in the defence of individual liberty.

The Concept of *Ordo*

The central and defining concern of the Freiburg School (and, subsequently, of all German neo-liberals) was 'order', the set of institutional-legal rules for a free society of essentially self-reliant decision-makers whose actions are controlled and coordinated by market competition. The Freiburg scholars focused on the underlying ordering principles that allow the millions of interdependent actors in a modern industrial society to interact. They preferred the spontaneous order of the market, but based on legally secured private property, to order created by command from above. They often used the Latin word *ordo*, which alluded to the Roman philosophical concept that described that state of civil(ised) society in which free men of good will could go about their legal business to good effect. It also alluded to the medieval Christian concept of a natural, harmonious state of a society aspiring to the realisation of natural law. The ideal of *ordo*, as the opposite of chaos and anarchy, has a long history in European (and, incidentally, East Asian) philosophy. The concept became controversial only when Karl Marx attacked the 'bourgeois-legal order' as a straightjacket put on society to defend capitalism. Many, though not all, Marxists preached a legal relativism that the German *ordo* liberals condemned outright as destructive of the very foundations of capitalist competition, freedom and prosperity (Kamenka, Brown & Tay, 1978). More recently, Hayek has pointed out again that the concept of 'order' need not have the connotation of hierarchy, formal organisation or authority (Hayek, 1973:35–54). He explicitly revived the notion that human instincts need to be disciplined in social and economic life by an order of ethical norms and conventions and by competition. The notion of an order that is not deliberately created was of course originally made popular by Adam Smith with the metaphor of the 'invisible hand'.

In 1936, Böhm, Eucken and Grossmann-Doerth got together to write an 'Ordo Manifesto' in which they laid the intellectual basis for their subsequent work (reprinted in English translation in Peacock & Willgerodt, 1989a:15–26). This document was written in reaction to the failures of the Weimar Republic, when the young German democracy had fallen prey to the ruthless power play of rent-seeking monopolies, cartels and unions and when high foreign debt, internal rigidities and lack of competition had helped to destroy democratic freedoms. The starting point for the three Freiburg scholars was the work of David Hume and Adam Smith, the great moral philosophers of the Scottish Enlightenment. They asked how the ideals of the Scottish liberal tradition could be practiced in a modern industrial society with oligopolies, technical innovation and a democratic process that was likely to be dominated by organised supplier interests. The Ordo Manifesto decried the relativism of the Historic School, which knew no ultimate values and objectives, and the fatalism of the socialists in the face of what they saw as deterministic laws of historic evolution.

The Freiburgers thus set out to develop a concept of what the modern state must do to maintain freedom and prosperity in the face of powerful vested interests. Theirs was a program 'to return law and economics to their proper place . . . [based on] . . . rational thought . . . Only the inwardly weak man sees reason as a threat, becomes uncertain and divided within himself because of it and, out of fear of the sober world of established facts and reason, rushes headlong into the intoxication of irrational, into feverish ecstasy' (Ordo Manifesto, in Peacock & Willgerodt, 1989a:22–3). In short, they chose to confront the problems of the time with an economic rationalism based on a commitment to freedom. Eucken in 1948 went so far as to postulate that 'economic policy ought to bring about the free, natural order that God has intended' (Peacock & Willgerodt, 1989a:34). He approved of Kant's statement that only free people could develop proper morality. The three founding fathers of the Freiburg School strove for freedom constrained by the rule of law so as to protect the individual against arbitrary actions of others. At the same time, they favoured the freedom of competition to promote prosperity (Eucken, 1952:360).

The *ordo* liberals understood that the various components of the economic system are closely interdependent. Interventions in one market tend to detract from the functioning of many other markets and activities, denying to many who are not directly affected by the intervention the realisation of their aspirations in indirect ways. This is why burgeoning *ad hoc* intervention leads to a gradual decay in overall efficiency and economic growth. Therefore, the 'treatment of all practical politico-legal and politico-economic questions must be keyed to the idea of the economic constitution' (Ordo Manifesto, in Peacock & Willgerodt, 1989a:23). By this they meant a reliable set of unwritten and written rules to ensure that competing decision-makers are able to decide freely, self-reliantly, and without specific government interference. They developed a cohesive vision of a stable framework of rules for the competitive game and pleaded for a government strong enough to prevent the anarchy of political power-play among well-connected interest groups. If government failed to defend the rules of the competitive game and got caught up in interventionist favouritism, then economic freedom and prosperity, and ultimately democracy itself, would be destroyed. The object lesson of the self-destruction of the Weimar democracy was thus the motivation and the starting point for the Freiburg analysis.

From the beginning, the Freiburg School explicitly addressed the permanent tension between the individual and the state. Differing from those whom they sometimes labelled 'Manchester liberals', who ignored the state as far as possible and at best saw it as an enemy of individual freedom, the Freiburgers tackled head-on the question of what constitutes good government. They explicitly asked how the government could defend the common, long-term interest in economic and social freedom within an industrial society with vested interests.[3]

---

3. Interestingly, the *ordo* liberal conclusions about good government were the direct opposite of the answers that the Australian consensus found in response to the same question in the late 19th and early 20th century. Whereas the Freiburgers stressed violations of freedom and the power-play of interest groups as the **causes** of social and economic failure in Germany, the Great Australian consensus from the Deakin era onwards had seen interest group politics and interference with individual freedoms as the **solution**: selective immigration, all-round protection, and redistribution through the arbitration system and the welfare state became the central pillars of governance (Kelly, 1992:1–12). Not the law, not ordering principles and self-motivated competition from below, but legislation and constructivist designs imposed from above were seen as the solution for social problems. The Australian solution was not the pursuit of happiness by self-reliance of free citizens within the rule of law, but collective action to serve individuals who were demanding state hand-outs and protection. Only from the late 1970s onwards has the Australian consensus begun to crumble, and insights similar to those of the Freiburgers in the wake of the Weimar fiasco have begun to spread.

The members of the Freiburg School and many other German liberals had great reservations from the outset about the collectivism of National Socialism. Some of them were involved with the resistance movement that was planning a new system of government after the (lost) war (known as the Erwin-von-Beckerath Circle). Much of this work, done in secret, was essential in laying the intellectual foundations for the re-emergence of a liberal civil society in Germany after the war.

The Constitutive Principles of a Liberal Order

The analytical approach and the central themes of *ordo* liberalism were inspired by the deplorable performance of economic policy during the inter-war period. The school based its views on the lessons of history rather than abstract modelling. The sub-title to Chapter 3 of the German original of Eucken's *Foundations* (1940:69) characterises their approach to scientific analysis: 'Not Distancing Oneself from Reality, but Penetrating it'. With this in mind, the neo-liberals formulated a new position on the relationship between history and social theory in order to create the intellectual foundations for limiting economic and political power and for defending a free society against privilege. Indeed, they considered this the essential task of government.

Eucken espoused an evolutionary view of social history. He therefore studied not only the rules that facilitate a rise in living standards (evolution within a given system of rules), but also other systems of rules and their effect on living standards (comparative systems). Yet Eucken was adamant that a body of precise economic theory was needed to analyse the issue. In asserting this, he was opposed to the German Historical School which had, for all practical purposes, decided against theory by postulating what was logically impossible, namely, that a perfect and complete description of history had to be completed before any theory could be formulated. The Historical School had asserted that, so far, economic theory had been of no use to the formulation of policy and that government intervention was needed to solve social problems. Eucken, in contrast, was intensely interested in a style of government that preserves freedom.

Eucken did not subscribe to economic theory as a pursuit for its own sake. He and other members in the Freiburg tradition did not engage in model building based on elegant but unrealistic assumptions and would not consider economic theory in isolation from the wider concerns of society. Eucken shared Lord Robbins's view that 'in the excitement of perfecting our instruments of analysis, we have tended to neglect a study of the framework which they assume' (cited approvingly in Eucken, 1948/65:197).[4]

Eucken started his analysis with the following considerations:

> If we were looking down on the world and its amazing swarm of human beings, on the variety of employments, the different patterns of related activities, and on the streams of goods, the first question we would ask is 'what is the order or system underlying all this?' ... Does one central authority direct everyday life, or do countless single individuals make their own decisions? If many individual economic units thought they make their plans independently, [but] are dependent on and exchange with one another . . . , then the question arises as to the form of the system of exchange relationships. What are the rules of the game? (Eucken, 1992:80–1)

Eucken stipulated the following key 'constitutive principles' (or fundamental institutions) that have to be ensured to obtain a well-functioning market economy:

- **private property**;
- **freedom of contract**;
- **liability** for one's commitments and actions;
- **open markets** (freedom of entry and exit);
- **monetary stability**, i.e. the provision of inflation-free money; and
- **steadiness of economic policy**.

The first three principles are close to what the political economists of the Scottish Enlightenment, from David Hume to Adam Smith, considered to be the basic institutions of a competitive capitalist economy. The classical political economists understood that private property alone can create the necessary incentives for innovation and risk taking, as well as for securing the individual liberty of 'citizens of property'. They also knew that free contracts were at the very basis of the market system of voluntary exchange and cooperation which guarantees the best development and utilisation of knowledge, and

---

4. Eucken drew heavily on philosophers like Edmund Husserl, when he developed his method of 'isolating abstraction' (1992:107) or as 'abstraction of significant salient features' (1992:332n). He contrasted this to 'generalising abstraction' that seeks to identify what is common to many phenomena. Instead, he sought to learn the important lessons from a limited number of case studies, drawing on *a priori* inductive reasoning.

that liability (as represented by, for example, the common law of tort) was an essential ingredient of a market system that ordered individual actions. Eucken added further principles because a modern democracy, with concentrated industrial and labour interests and much greater government influence than had been imagined at the dawn of the industrial age, needed better defences of the market system if it was to function properly. Eucken's additions were no doubt inspired by the poor economic record and the interest-group politics of the 1920s, with runaway inflation at the beginning of the decade and opportunistic interventionism and lobbying throughout the Weimar Republic. This had eroded the proper functioning of the market system and impeded the spontaneous coordination of independent decisions of countless individuals. The result was a feeling of widespread failure and, eventually, the loss of freedom and peace under the National Socialist regime.

In stipulating the principle of open markets, Eucken made it clear that competition is a public good that the government must defend. The prohibition against closing-off markets serves as the control mechanism which prevents the institution of private property from leading to economic and social abuse. To him, 'the social question' (concerns with welfare and poverty) and popular dissatisfaction with the market economy were the results of insufficient competition, reflecting the failure of the government to set and preserve the framework of a truly competitive order, for example when it tolerated cartels. Eucken also argued that price-level stability was a fundamental ingredient of a market order because it alone permits rational economic decisions by individual market participants who are guided by relative price changes; these price signals would be distorted or disguised by inflation. Eucken also espoused steadiness of economic policy on the grounds that the frequent changes of discretionary policy confound individuals' expectations and their plans, preventing them from realising their goals.[5]

These fundamental constitutive principles should be assured by government in what Eucken called 'order policy' (*Ordnungspolitik*). In many ways, Eucken anticipated the discovery by social historian Douglass North that such institutional arrangements are essential for

---

5. The *ordo* liberal catalogue of institutions of a free market economy was taken up by the Australian Coalition parties in their *Fightback!* program in 1992 which was aimed at tackling low economic dynamism and interest-group dominance in economic policy not dissimilar to the Weimar Republic's decline (Liberal/National Parties, 1991:26–9).

modern capitalism and sustained economic growth, and that the state enjoys important economies of scale in protecting institutions such as private property (North & Thomas, 1973). Eucken concluded that, once these constitutional principles were assured, the government should leave competitive market processes alone: not the untrammelled *laissez faire* of anarcho-capitalism, but *laissez faire* within a legal framework.

Eucken's conclusions about the basic design of economic policy were shared by his co-founders. As early as 1933, Grossmann-Doerth drew attention to what he called the 'self-created law of the business community' who had developed their own rules and regulations that were ratified by the legislative and regulatory process and tended to undermine the competitive order. Böhm drew on his experience in the German Cartel Office to castigate private attempts to close off markets by the formation of cartels. He opposed the then widely held view that cartels had to be tolerated under the general freedom of contract. He pointed out that cartels totally violated the freedom of third parties to compete. And, like Eucken, he deplored the fact that private closure of markets often received public support through regulation. In many respects, Böhm and Eucken anticipated Mancur Olson (1982) and some of the contributions of the public-choice school.

A central tenet of the *ordo* liberal school was that competition must be recognised as a constitutive element of the economic system, which needs protection, nurture and support by the law. The *ordo* liberals saw government as the provider and enforcer of such law. Their experience would have led them to withhold endorsement for more recent tendencies for private provision of the law (Benson, 1990). The Freiburg School advocated strong but limited government: strong enough to hold out against monopolies and pressure groups, yet limited by the rule of the law *(Rechtsstaat)*. The German neo-liberals pointed out that, to give legal status to the freedom to compete, it was necessary to think in terms of economic systems and of shaping economic systems by legal means. This could not be done within a 'value-free' system of purely positive economics. It was necessary to stipulate a basic value, namely, freedom. Böhm developed the concept of an economic constitution on that basis. He recognised that, in view of the fundamental conflict between freedom and power, the rules governing private autonomy in a market system and those securing the control of its use through competition must be considered as mutually complementary. Böhm dwelt on the structural similarity between his concept of an economic constitution and the political constitution of a free society in dealing with autonomy and power. Under a political constitution it is of course necessary to grant autonomy to those who make the laws. But since legislative autonomy tends to provide opportunities to abuse power, a long tradition, from Locke and Montesquieu onwards, elaborated a sophisticated combination of constitutional checks and balances to prevent, or at least constrain, this abuse.

The Achievements of *Ordo* Liberalism

The basic philosophy of *ordo* liberalism renders it much more akin to classical political economy, which was committed to values like freedom and their institutional support, than to 20th-century mainstream Anglo-American economics, which concentrates on purely positive economics and is devoid of institutions (Hutchison, 1979:433). In this sense, Robbins's comparison of classical political economy with modern economic theorising also applies to the *ordo* liberal school: 'Their conception of the System of Economic Freedom was surely a conception of something more rough and ready, something much more dynamic and real than these exquisite laboratory models' (1952/61:16). Speculation about institutions must involve value judgments, because institutions are never value-free. The *ordo* liberal position thus reflects a pragmatic interest in economic policy and makes an explicit choice against interventionism and collectivism by advocating an institutional framework conducive to freedom and prosperity.

This policy orientation is well documented by the policy advice from Freiburg after the Second World War. Eucken and Böhm served as advisers first to the Western military governments and thereafter to Ludwig Erhard, who began his career as the head of the Economic Administration Office of the British and American occupation zones. Later they were appointed to the Advisory Board of the Federal Republic's Ministry of Economics when it was founded in 1948. Eucken became the leading intellectual figure in the pro-market majority of the Advisory Board (Giersch, 1988:8). That majority espoused the optimistic view that reforms would lead to a much more efficient economy and a 'productivity breakout', a stance that Erhard shared and helped to translate into reality. Böhm became a member of federal parliament and was able to exert great influence on Germany's anti-trust legislation, creating a pro-competitive trade practices authority (the Cartel Office), which interest groups have not yet been able to capture. This success is due partly to the independence of the German Cartel Office and its commitment to the basic principle of free competition, and partly to the relative openness of the German economy to international competition. In any event, the formative period of post-war West Germany bears the strong imprint of the Freiburg School. But since the mid-1960s that influence has waned.

Apart from this practical influence, hindsight reveals at least five major analytical achievements of the school.

First, it formulated a well founded, institutionally-based criticism of collectivist economic planning. This was done independently of the Austrian School, in the 1930s and 1940s, when most mainstream economists still considered central planning theoretically feasible.

Second, the School demonstrated the importance of institutions to the functioning of a market system. This was in complete contrast to conventional economics at the time, which was blind to the importance of institutions. Post-war mainstream theorists had almost nothing to say about public versus private property or microeconomic reform to enhance the efficiency of the market system. On the contrary, they often saw economic coordination by bureaucratic planning as inherently superior to the competitive chaos of the market place. The *ordo* liberals argued in favour of legislation that sets the rules for private competition; but, unlike contemporary, evolutionary constitutional economics, they did not analyse matters in terms of a choice among differing sets of rules or the evolution of rules.

Third, the school, with its fundamental commitment to freedom, had fewer problems in accepting and elaborating on the inevitable normative nature of institutions than more recent approaches.

Fourth, the school was highly sceptical of the possibility of directing market processes. It certainly took Anglo-Saxon mainstream economics much longer to recognise the limitations of 'rational intervention' at both the micro- and the macro-level.

Finally, great emphasis was placed on the interdependence between the various sub-systems of the social order that must be kept in mind when structuring and adapting social institutions. The conviction that civil and economic freedoms are interdependent, for example, played a big role during the heated public discussion on the future political and economic order of Germany during the first years after the war. Böhm then denied vehemently that it would be possible to combine a constitution for a democratic government under the rule of law with socialist central planning (Böhm, 1950/80). This was one application of Eucken's important proposition that there is an 'interdependence of orders'.

The contributions of the Freiburg School do not form one consistent, unchangeable doctrine (a concept alien to the liberal spirit of the Freiburgers). One can say that they form part of the long liberal tradition. They focused more on institutions and the law than did the classical liberal writers, and they differ in some respects from modern Anglo-Saxon liberalism. They certainly had more faith in what good, lawful government and competent civil servants can achieve for a free society than, say, economists like Friedrich von Hayek or Milton Friedman, let alone contemporary public-choice analysts. Their, strictly limited, faith in the possibility of good government prompted them to think more clearly, more pragmatically and more carefully about the design of constitutional and legal arrangements that make for good government. In a world in which much imperfect — even outright bad — government exists and from which government will not disappear, the *ordo* liberal tradition may serve as an inspiration to reform government. At the very least, the German neo-liberals did much to demonstrate how institutions determine human behaviour and that social reform has to begin by recasting institutions and confining the sphere of collective control. One lesson certainly is that market reforms which are not bound by the right institutions can be undone quickly again (as has been happening to the Reagan and Thatcher reforms).

Subsequent Developments

Although the academic and political dominance of the Freiburg School faded somewhat after Eucken's death and with the gradual adoption of Anglo-American theoretical economics in Germany, the tradition lives on. It survives in the disciplines of law and economics at different locations and with the same commitment to individuality which, from the beginning, prevented the emergence of a narrow and monolithic doctrine.

The outstanding example of a scholar who continued the *ordo* liberal tradition with stimulating new challenges was undoubtedly **Friedrich A. von Hayek**. The continuity stands out clearly when one reads Böhm's 'Rule of Law in a Market Economy' (1966/89a) alongside Hayek's 'Rechtsordnung und Handelsordnung' ('Order of Law and Order of Actions') (1967b). The latter marks the beginning of an intellectual development for Hayek, in which he deepened the analysis of the relationship between the market system as a spontaneous order and its constitutive system of rules, including private law. Hayek's analysis culminated in his trilogy *Law, Legislation and Liberty*, which clearly reveals a 'Freiburg inspiration' to those familiar with earlier Freiburg writings on law and the market economy.

Hayek contributed stimulating innovative insights from his basis of Austrian subjectivism and his emphasis on the knowledge problem: the insight that limitations of specific, productive knowledge are at the base of economic scarcity. Eucken had distanced himself from the Historical School by adopting, at least to some extent, neo-classical economics and, with it, rationalist elements; but Hayek broke with the neo-classical approach and found new theoretical insights into the use of knowledge by competitors and the evolution of appropriate institutions.

Hayek's theory of competition as a 'discovery procedure' has its theoretical and constitutional equivalent in a competition policy that is based on the fundamental concept of the 'freedom to compete'. Hayek inspired competition policies that favour discovery and innovation and that differ from the well-known 'structure-conduct-performance paradigm' of the Harvard School. In this, Hayek came fairly close to the views of Eucken and his disciples, but he also broke with the neo-classical orientation of anti-trust policy towards efficiency, stressing that competition was important not only for a dynamic economy but also for individual freedom.

In jurisprudence, the continuity and further development of *ordo* liberalism is now closely linked with the name of **Ernst-Joachim Mestmäcker**, the most distinguished disciple of Böhm in both consti-tutional and anti-trust law (e.g. Mestmäcker, 1973/74 and 1980).

Seen from a different angle, the German *ordo* liberals drew attention to the 'soft, cultural technology' (the institutions, the rules, the individual attitudes) that society has to develop and nurture in the interest of freedom and prosperity. The moral and institutional foundations of prosperity may be less obvious than the 'hardware of development', like capital goods and natural resources, but they are more important for economic growth. Institutions help to reduce the costs of exchange and innovation, and profoundly affect the gains from specialisation that can be realised in any particular society. Where uncertainty is great, reflecting a lack of trust between potential business partners, there will be little credit and many potentially wealth-creating transac-tions are simply not made. In an era when prosperity increasingly depends on the growing division of labour, services, fast-changing products, innovation and quick responses to market opportunities, the institutional foundations are becoming ever more important.

This is why the basic Freiburg message holds great relevance now.

The German neo-liberals came close to fleshing out what Milton Friedman later stipulated as the role of government:

> A government which maintained law and order, defined property rights, served as a means whereby we could modify property rights and other rules of the economic game, adjudicated disputes about the interpretation of the rules, enforced contracts, promoted competition, provided a monetary framework, engaged in activities to counter technical monopolies and to overcome neighbourhood effects widely regarded as sufficiently important to justify government intervention, and which supplemented private charity and the private family in protecting the irresponsible, whether madman or child — such a government would clearly have important functions to perform. The consistent liberal is not an anarchist. (Friedman, 1962:34)

III. THE WELFARE STATE AND A LIBERAL ORDER

One policy issue to which different *ordo* liberals have given different answers is the extent to which the state should provide for the welfare of those who gain little from competition. This revolves around what has been called in Germany 'the social question'.[6] Eucken's first reaction was to say that the social question had changed dramatically when compared with the early industrialisation of the 19th century. As already mentioned, he diagnosed an unsatisfactory distribution of income as the consequence of insufficient competition and mono-polies, which confer income advantages on some and deprive others of opportunity. He maintained that case-by-case remedies for social ills were counterproductive and that 'people in depend-ency or need have a right to demand an order [that] enables them to live a humane life' (Eucken, 1952:314–15, our translation). He saw that redistributional policy interferes with the ordering principles of

---

6. The notion of the 'social question' creates a much closer link between individual welfare and the wage, with state provision of income a much more subsidiary concern than in the Anglo-Saxon tradition where the term 'welfare state' often implies that governments have the responsibility for individual welfare. In Germany, the role of the market and of economic development is taken to be central to the material welfare of the family. After Bismarck's welfare reforms, the state was always seen, much more than in Anglo-Saxon countries, only as a 'provider of last resort'.

free-market competition, which requires responsibility for oneself and liability for one's actions. A basic concept of *ordo* liberalism is, after all, that economic policy must stick to the rules of competition in the interest of favourable outcomes for society as a whole, irrespective of the consequences for specific groups, persons or projects.

Nevertheless, Eucken recognised social policy as a secondary 'regulatory principle', on the grounds that gross social imbalances were prejudicial to the smooth working of the market economy. He supported measures to protect workers and saw the task of unions to ensure workers' living standards and material security. But he kept coming back to the importance of a well-functioning market economy if individuals were to be protected from poverty and provided with material security. 'Everything depends on whether the thinking in terms of an order, the concept of a free order, is incorporated also into social attitudes. If the relevant decision makers strive simultaneously for order and liberty, then it is possible to build a free, ordered society which fulfils the great European intellectual tradition, the principle of a humane society' (1952:323–4, our translation). Eucken of course recognised that the market process leads to unequal outcomes that have to be generally accepted. His concern with the 'social question' focused mainly on the eradication of absolute poverty as opposed to correcting income inequalities. This is why he stressed open competition as a means of speeding up growth and spreading opportunity to those at the bottom of the income range.

Some writers close to the Freiburg School early on attacked the penchant of the post-war German political system for redistribution. Thus, Wilhelm Röpke warned as early as 1950 that income redistribution and subsidies had gone too far. He warned of the powerful populist pressures that entrench the growth of transfer payments and spoke of the 'transfer state' long before public-choice theory discovered this phenomenon as a systematic weakness of the present form of unconstrained democracy (for his arguments, in English, see Röpke, 1948, 1960).

Other writers, who were on the whole close to the ideas of the Freiburg School, thought that a modern capitalist, democratic society had to engage in a degree of redistribution. Thus, Alfred Müller-Armack, who was influential as the long-term top civil servant in the Economics Ministry, coined the notion of the 'social market economy' and argued for public welfare provision. As the West German economy emerged from the immediate post-war period and welfare pressure groups formed again, the inconsistency between free competition and redistribution became apparent and the borderline between *ordo*-liberal theory and 'social-market' practice was shifted away from reliance on genuine market allocation. The commitment to redistribution thus gradually undid the heritage of *ordo* liberalism and contributed to the gradual reemergence of a regulatory-corporatist culture (Bernholz, 1979; Giersch et al., 1992).

Many German liberal writers have warned that the commitment to public welfare is the undoing of the market economy which the *ordo* liberals had envisaged, and that the gradual slide from the 'economic miracle' into 'Euro-sclerosis' is tied to that change. Thus, **Walter Hamm**, a co-editor of the *Ordo* Yearbook, wrote a much-cited article in 1981 warning that the welfare state had reached its limit (translated in Peacock & Willgerodt, 1989a:171–94). He demonstrated that 'measures that are intended to be socially beneficial . . . have anti-social consequences' (p.171). And he returned to Eucken's original position when he showed that the failure of the government to stick to the principles of 'order policy' was often the very cause of welfare dependency. The need for welfare transfers is increased, for example, when the government causes inflation, when it encourages a 'risk-avoidance and claims mentality', regulates prices, raises unemployment by labour-market regulations or pursues egalitarian policies that destroy incentives to work and save. Hamm saw very clearly what Eucken had predicted, namely, that the welfare state gradually inculcates behaviour patterns that erode continued prosperity and freedom. Only a return to the fundamental principles of an economic order can remedy the consequences of that.

In the spirit and the tradition of *ordo* liberalism, Walter Hamm called for a reorientation of policy from the widespread notion that 'social well-being can originate only from the state' (p.189). He suggested that an end has to be put to the continuing advance of the welfare state by a number of measures:

- explain to the electorate that individual freedom (and freedom from bureaucratic surveillance) is not feasible once all-embracing state 'care' has become the norm;

- mobilise popular unease with the burden of comprehensive redistribution policies in order to induce politicians to resist the lobbying of redistributional interest groups, and raise public awareness of the long-run effects of social-welfare programs;

- reform the tax system, especially marginal income taxes, to enhance the will to work;

- remove the incentives against job creation from wage and tax policy and make taxation neutral in its impact on different categories of labour;

- move welfare provision from the central government to local governments or community groups, while retaining compulsory insurance against major risks to individual welfare (e.g. accidents, or health);

- ensure that privileged groups of employees who hold critical positions (e.g. pilots) are not allowed to enter into contracts that burden particular firms with high labour costs, since this might cause unemployment for many others;

- attack egalitarian wages policies by unions on the grounds that this destroys the jobs of many low-productivity workers; and

- return to the basic principles of *ordo* policy, namely, to adhere to the maxim of 'No Favours All Round' and the fight against inflation.

IV. ECONOMIC ORDER AND OPENNESS

The original Freiburg School developed its basic position between the 1930s and the 1950s, at a time when national economic systems were relatively closed: spatially closed towards the competitive influences of international trade and movements of capital, skilled people and enterprises, and technically closed towards new products and processes due to relatively slow innovation. This induced the Freiburgers to seek strong support for proper competitiveness from the government and legislation. It has been pointed out that nowadays, in a system that is open to international competition and innovation, a strong government is no longer all that necessary to ensure a proper competitive order (Giersch, 1988:5). Worldwide competition and innovation are now breaking monopolies, thus reducing the need for strong government such as the Freiburg School had advocated.

There is certainly some compelling truth in this argument. Openness has to be considered crucial for a well-functioning market economy. In any case, the 'constitutive principle' of open markets (freedom of entry and exit) in the *ordo* liberal catalogue includes the obligation of the government to keep markets open to international competitors and to innovators. More important, the growing internationalisation of national economies and more rapid technical change are now giving the economic order a new role:

- With growing globalisation, as capital, high technical and entrepreneurial skills and technology are increasingly mobile between countries, the attainment of international competitiveness is the task of those production factors that cannot move easily across borders — such as labour and government administrations (Kasper, 1992b). In their own self-interest, governments have to attract and retain mobile production factors by enabling these to earn competitive rates of return within their jurisdiction. This is now leading increasingly to international administrative 'systems competition' in which the regulatory-legal system of government and taxation play a focal role. In other words, globalisation now creates new demands for a competition-friendly economic order.

- In a world of fast technical innovation, in which fixed costs and risks are frequently high and firms are under pressure to recoup innovation costs quickly by marketing a new product immediately on a global scale, there is a high premium on policy settings that provide clear, transparent rules. Technical and industrial change can be managed better by business and others if they can operate within a firm, reliable order. The likelihood of innovation, and of commercial success with innovation, greatly depends on a framework of formal and informal rules and market-friendly institutions.

We therefore must conclude that, far from having become less relevant, the *ordo* liberal approach now deserves heightened attention. In the dynamic modern world economy, extrapolation from the past is less reliable. Decision-makers in business therefore have to depend more heavily for their success on a general, simple and stable order. Reliable, expedient rules with low compliance costs can greatly cut the costs of doing business and of innovating. Institutional innovation is therefore becoming a powerful new tool of international competition. And institutional reform has to begin with the realisation that governments must transform themselves from rulers exercising power into support organisations servicing competing market activities (Kasper, 1992b).

Policy makers should also realise that business competitors require a consistent set of compatible sub-orders. Reforms are hindered by inherent contradictions between areas that are regulated and areas that are open to competition. Thus it is necessary to deregulate **all** product and factor markets, since partial deregulation leads to distortive price signals and misallocations of effort. Eucken's insight into the interdependence of sub-orders makes for comprehensive reform. Anything short of this hinders competition in an open world.

V. ORDER AND ECONOMIC REFORM

The *ordo* liberal call in post-war Germany for concentrating the limited capabilities of government on the essentials and for abandoning the diversions of specific *ad hoc* interventions ensured the success of transforming the *dirigiste* policy of the Third Reich and the post-war military administration. By making order the central concern of economic policy, German reformers ensured that the task remained manageable and that the millions of private decision-makers were able to understand the new rules. They soon acted self-reliantly and gave up pleading for special favours. This lesson of history seems important at a time when reforms of the economic system are a widespread phenomenon in East and West.

The notion of a fundamental order, the violation of which erodes the benefits of competitive capitalism, needs to be revived especially in societies where the institutional foundations of capitalism have been taken for granted. All too often, deficiencies in the underlying socio-economic order have been allowed to evolve. All too often, the deleterious and cumulative side effects of activist politicking have been ignored. This has led to the market economy yielding unsatisfactory results in terms of growth and equity. The reaction of the democratic system has all too often been to intervene and patch up the failures with more interventions. Thus, long-lasting inflation, a violation of one of Eucken's fundamental principles, has created an unintended and undesirable redistribution of incomes and wealth, and the welfare state has intervened to remedy the consequences. But such interventions further undermined the inherent capability of the market economy to perform in socially desired ways. Only a return to fundamental principles and control of the interventionist urge can avert the cumulative slide into a 'mixed economy' that fails to perform satisfactorily and that ultimately leads to a widespread unease not only with the capitalist system, but with democracy. The repair of the capitalist market economy therefore seems urgent.

As already mentioned, the urgency is now enhanced by the growing international mobility of certain production factors, like financial, physical and knowledge capital, enterprise and entire firms. These production factors are increasingly shopping around for the socio-economic system that ensures the best rates of return and lowest risks. The government has a central role in shaping the competitive conditions that attract or repel mobile production factors. We are therefore moving into an epoch of 'international systems competition', when market-friendly orders will attract productivity-enhancing, mobile capital and skills as never before and when interventionist regimes will lose out, until they, too, learn to evolve appropriate rules to succeed in the competitive game (Kasper, 1992b).

If the now widespread unease with government, markets and business is to be addressed, it seems necessary to begin by proclaiming the rules of the fundamental order. The capitalist system should be repaired, not by a tacit, pragmatic drift into a reformed economic system, but by starting with a clear strategic proclamation of the basic principles. In old, decaying capitalist market systems, the principles may be taken for granted and their central importance to the functioning of the market economy may therefore be almost forgotten. In formerly socialist or corporatist systems, the essential foundations of competitive capitalism may be unknown and may therefore be unwittingly violated, as societies struggle to build a capitalist system.

Therefore, a programmatic affirmation of the institutional principles can greatly ease the costs of transition to a new set of the basic rules. During the process of microeconomic reform and the transformation of the economic system, the development and propagation of a simple, consistent, market-friendly economic order can fulfil the following important functions:

- It can help to alert all participants in the economy that the underlying rules and incentives have been decaying at great cost to society. This may have come about gradually and imperceptibly in the face of prevalent statism, pressure-group lobbying, and rent-seeking at the expense of the common good. Starting from basic principles, then, has the advantage of mobilising the will of all involved to face up to the costs of reform. The principles embody a vision of society for which one can gain electoral support, which would not be forthcoming for the technicalities of reform.

- Spelling out of the basic principles of a competitive order can serve to educate the many participants in politics and the bureaucracy about the need to conduct market-friendly reforms despite possible short-run pain. Focusing on the principles of a liberal order can avoid costly inconsistencies, accidents and reversals in the reform process. All participants in policy making can be forced to concentrate on the essentials of a well-functioning market economy.

- A commitment to simple, clear rules will help to coordinate the various levels of government, including State and local governments, which have the capacity to frustrate federal policies to enhance competitiveness. The framework of a competitive society should explicitly encourage State and local administrations to compete with each other for productive resources. In this way all involved learn to act in competition-friendly ways.

- Inconsistencies between different parts of the government are always confusing and may destroy productivity. A commitment to a simple framework of basic rules will avoid malcoordination between the various arms of government and will ensure that the various sub-orders concerning different markets remain consistent and mutually supportive.[7]

- Governments are also liable to inconsistencies over time. That often imposes heavy costs on private decision-makers who trusted the word of officials in making their own long-term plans. A clearly spelled-out catalogue of the 'Basic Commandments of Market-Friendly Principles' forces ministers and bureaucrats to resist the ever-present temptations of ad-hocery and steers them away from the notion that politics is inevitably no more than the 'art of the possible'.

- When the underlying economic system is being transformed by pragmatic piecemeal microeconomic reform, the danger exists of leads and lags between the many private decision makers who have to adjust to the new rules. As already mentioned, leads and lags in learning about the individual consequences of a new policy game-plan can be costly to economic growth. In this respect, too, an explicit commitment to an economic order can serve an essential coordinating function and thus reduce the costs of transformation.

- When liberalisation and globalisation after a long era of inward-looking policy lead to exposure to international competition (as is the case in Australia in the 1990s), it may be possible to use an

---

7. For example, a reform strategy, like that of New Zealand in the 1980s, which deregulated product and capital markets and at the same time re-regulated labour markets, violated a basic principle of *ordo* liberalism. Not surprisingly, it led to costly accidents. The same dangers loom if specific markets are exempted from the rules of competition, be it agriculture or motor cars, or when strict political control is combined with economic freedom, as in China. Inconsistencies are likely to hinder the effectiveness of the system and may sooner or later endanger the reform process.

explicit, positive statement of the basic rules also as a signalling device on the international scene. The world may then learn faster about the intended change. This is likely to strengthen investor confidence at home and abroad and will thus assist in the early success of the reforms.

In the 1990s, reformers will need to proceed with a coherent strategy. They will not be able to implement reforms piecemeal, that is, only as and when it is pragmatically and tactically feasible. Reform is much easier if the reformers commit themselves from the beginning to an explicit strategic vision of where the reforms are ultimately headed. Then, the inevitable tactical mishaps and political debates about details are less likely to cast doubt on the overall strategy of transforming the system.

VI. CONCLUSION

When a competition-friendly order has been implemented, sight must never be lost of the main purpose of 'order policy', namely, to ensure that enterprise is directed away from seeking a return on its assets by securing politically sanctioned rents and privileges. The overriding goal is to steer all producers into sustained, though possibly uncomfortable, creative unease, which forces them to compete and defend their market positions by process and product innovation, cutting costs and creating new market niches.

A liberal socio-economic order has of course benefits that go far beyond material prosperity. By giving scope to self-reliance and enhancing the conditions for individual success, reforms can inspire optimism and, as the *ordo* liberals pointed out time and again, they certainly hold out the promise of freedom. Only when people have a good chance of realising their self-chosen purposes will they support the system of democratic government and competitive capitalism.

References and Further Reading

The references below are not exhaustive, but provide a list of further reading for English-speakers who wish to pursue the central themes of *ordo* liberalism and institutional economics. The central marketplace for the evolving ideas on these issues is the *Ordo Yearbook*, which has been published annually since 1948, many with articles in English. To the best of our knowledge, no Australian library subscribes to *Ordo*.

Balogh, T. (1950), *Germany: An Experiment in 'Planning' by the 'Free' Price Mechanism*, Basil Blackwell, Oxford.

Barry, N. (1989), 'Political and Economic Thought of German Neo-Liberals', pp. 105–124 in A. Peacock & H. Willgerodt (eds) (1989b), *German Neo-Liberals and the Social Market Economy*, Macmillan, London.

Baumol, W. (1990), 'Entrepreneurship: Productive, Unproductive and Destructive', *Journal of Political Economy* 98 (Oct.): 893–921.

Benson, B. (1990), *The Enterprise of Law*, Pacific Research Institute for Public Policy, San Francisco.

Bernholz, P. (1979), 'Freedom and Constitutional Order', *Journal of Institutional and Theoretical Economics* 135: 465–88.

—— (1983), 'Inflation and Monetary Constitutions in Historical Perspective', *Kyklos* 36: 397–419.

Böhm, F. (1950/80), 'Wirtschaftsordnung und Staatsverfassung', pp. 46–87 in E. Mestmäcker (ed.) (1980), *Freiheit und Ordnung in der Marktwirtschaft*, Nomos, Baden-Baden.

—— (1966/89a), 'The Rule of Law in a Market Economy', pp. 46–67 in A. Peacock & H. Willgerodt (eds) (1989a), *Germany's Social Market Economy: Origins and Evolution*, Macmillan, London.

—— (1979), 'Left-wing and Right-wing Approaches to the Market Economy', *Journal of Institutional and Theoretical Economics* 135.

Buchanan, J. (1988), 'Constitutional Imperatives for the 1990s: The Legal Order for a Free and Productive Economy', pp. 253–64 in A. Anderson & D. Bark (eds), *Thinking about America*, Hoover Institution Press, Stanford.

—— & G. Tullock (1965), *The Calculus of Consent*, University of Michigan Press, Ann Arbor.

Chen, K. (1988), 'The Economics and Non-Economics of Asia's Four Little Dragons', *University of Hong Kong Gazette* 35, Supplement, pp. 23–30.

Erhard, L. (1960), *Prosperity through Competition*, Thames Hudson, London (German original, 1958).

Eucken, W. (1951), *This Unsuccessful Age,* William Hodge, Edinburgh.

—— (1952), *Grundsätze der Wirtschaftspolitik,* Mohr Siebeck, Tübingen (published posthumously; though immensely influential on the Continent, 'Principles of Economic Policy' has never been translated into English).

—— (1948/65), 'On the Theory of the Centrally Administered Economy: An Analysis of the German Experiment', pp. 157–97 in M. Bornstein (ed.), *Comparative Economic Systems – Models and Cases,* Irwin, Homewood, Ill.

—— (1992), *The Foundations of Economics, History and Theory in the Analysis of Economic Reality,* Springer, New York & Heidelberg (German original: *Grundlagen der Nationalökonomie,* 1st ed., Gustav Fischer, Jena, 1940; 1st English edition: *Foundations of Economics,* William Hodge, Edinburgh, 1950).

Friedman, M. (1962), *Capitalism and Freedom,* Chicago University Press, Chicago.

Giersch, H. (1988), 'Liberal Reform in West Germany', *Ordo* 39: 3–16.

—— (1989), *The Ethics of Economic Freedom,* Centre for Independent Studies, Sydney.

——, K.-H. Paqué, & H. Schmieding (1992), *The Fading Miracle: Four Decades of Market Economy in Germany,* Cambridge University Press, Cambridge, UK.

Hayek, F. (1948), *Individualism and Economic Order,* Chicago University Press, Chicago.

—— (1960), *The Constitution of Liberty,* Chicago University Press, Chicago.

—— (1967a), 'The Principles of a Liberal Social Order', pp. 160–77 in F.A. Hayek, *Studies in Philosophy, Politics and Economics,* Routledge & Kegan Paul, London.

—— (1967b), 'Rechtsordnung und Handelsordnung', in Fakultät des Albert-Ludwigs-Universität Freiburg, *Zur Einheit des Rechts- und Stattswissenschaffen,* Karlsruhe, 1966/67.

—— (1973), *Rules and Order,* vol. 1 of *Law, Legislation and Liberty,* Routledge & Kegan Paul, London.

—— (1979), *The Political Order of a Free People,* vol. 3 of *Law, Legislation and Liberty,* Routledge & Kegan Paul, London.

—— (1992), *Why I Am Not a Conservative,* Centre for Independent Studies, Sydney.

Hutchison, T. (1979), 'Notes on the Effects of Economic Ideas on Policy: The Example of the German Social Market Economy', *Journal of Institutional and Theoretical Economics* 135: 426–41.

—— (1984), 'Institutionalist Economics Old and New', *Journal of Institutional and Theoretical Economics* 140: 20–9.

Kamenka, E., R. Brown & A. Tay (eds) (1978), *Law and Society: The Crisis in Legal Ideals*, Arnold, London.

Kasper, W. (1990), 'Firing Up the Little Dragons', *Economics Affairs* 11(1): 21–3.

—— (1992a), 'Competition and Growth: The Lessons of East Asia', pp. 279–304 in H. Giersch, *Money, Trade and Competition*, Springer Publishers, Heidelberg & New York.

—— (1992b), 'Advancing into the 21st Century: Visions and Challenges Facing the Downunder Economy', *Australian Economic Review* (December): 27–40.

Kelly, P. (1992), *The End of Certainty: The Story of the 1980s*, Allen & Unwin, Sydney.

Liberal/National Parties (1991), *Fightback! – It's Your Australia*, Canberra.

Ludwig Erhard Foundation (1980), *Standard Texts on the Social Market Economy*, G. Fischer, New York.

Mestmäcker, E.-J. (1973/74), 'Power, Law and Economic Constitution', *Law and State* 10: 117–32.

—— (1980), 'Competition Policy and Antitrust', *Journal of Institutional and Theoretical Economics* 136: 387–407.

Mises, L. von (1949), *Human Action*, William Hodge, Edinburgh.

North, D. (1990), *Institutions, Institutional Change, and Economic Performance*, Cambridge University Press, New York.

—— & R. Thomas (1973), *The Rise of the Western World: A New Economic History*, Cambridge University Press, Cambridge, UK.

Oliver, H. (1960), 'German Neo-Liberalism', *Quarterly Journal of Economics* 74: 117–49.

Olson, M. (1982), *The Rise and Decline of Nations*, Yale University Press, New Haven, Conn.

Peacock, A. & H. Willgerodt (eds) (1989a), *Germany's Social Market Economy: Origins and Evolution*, Macmillan, London.

—— (1989b), *German Neo-Liberals and the Social Market Economy*, Macmillan, London.

Robbins, L. (1952/61), *The Theory of Economic Policy*, Macmillan, London.

Röpke, W. (1948), *Civitas Humana, A Humane Order of Society*, William Hodge, London.

—— (1957), *Welfare, Freedom and Inflation*, Pall Mall Press, London.

—— (1960), *A Humane Economy: the Social Framework of the Free Market*, Henry Regnery, Chicago.

—— (1963), *Economics of the Free Society*, Henry Regnery Gateway, Chicago.

Rüstow, A. (1980), *Freedom or Domination: A Historical Critique of Civilisation*, Princeton University Press, Princeton (German originals, 1950 & 1957).

Scobie, G. & S. Lim (1992), 'Economic Reform: A Global Revolution', *Policy* (Spring): 2–7.

Sohmen, E. (1959), 'Competition and Growth – The Lesson of West Germany', *American Economic Review* 49: 986–1003 (see also the ensuing debate, *American Economic Review* 50: 1015–31).

Streit, M. (1987), 'Economic Order and Public Policy – Market, Constitution and the Welfare State', pp. 1–21 in R. Pethig & U. Schlieper (eds), *Efficiency, Institutions and Economic Policy*, Springer Publishers, Heidelberg, New York.

—— (1992a), 'Welfare Economics, Economic Order, and Competition', pp. 255–78 in H. Giersch (ed.), *Money, Trade, and Competition – Essays in Memory of Egon Sohmen*, Springer Publishers, Heidelberg, New York.

—— (1992b), 'Economic Order, Private Law and Public Policy: The Freiburg School of Law and Economics in Perspective', *Journal of Institutional and Theoretical Economics* 148(4): 675–704.

Tumlir, J. (1979), 'International Economic Order and Democratic Constitutionalism', *Ordo* 34: 71–83.

Vanberg, V. (1988), '"Ordnungstheorie" as Constitutional Economics – The German Conception of a Social Market Economy', *Ordo* 39: 17–32.